T0063506

Scritti Is Witty

Cormac G. McDermott BA MEconSc

Order this book online at www.trafford.com
or email orders@trafford.com

Most Trafford titles are also available at major online book retailers.

© Copyright 2014 Cormac G. McDermott BA MEconSc.
All rights reserved. No part of this publication may be reproduced, stored in a retrieval
system, or transmitted, in any form or by any means, electronic, mechanical, photocopying,
recording, or otherwise, without the written prior permission of the author.

Printed in the United States of America.

ISBN: 978-1-4907-3400-2 (sc)
ISBN: 978-1-4907-3399-9 (e)

Because of the dynamic nature of the Internet, any web addresses or links contained in
this book may have changed since publication and may no longer be valid. The views
expressed in this work are solely those of the author and do not necessarily reflect the
views of the publisher, and the publisher hereby disclaims any responsibility for them.

Any people depicted in stock imagery provided by Thinkstock are models,
and such images are being used for illustrative purposes only.
Certain stock imagery © Thinkstock. .

Trafford rev. 04/21/2014

www.trafford.com

North America & international
toll-free: 1 888 232 4444 (USA & Canada)
fax: 812 355 4082

Contents

Chapter 1

COMEDY SKETCHES

SCENE FROM A PHARMACY—ED HAS BUMPED INTO HIS OLD
SCHOOL PAL (STOOL).

ED: 'Hi there, Stool. I can't remember the last time I saw you. Are you back living in this area?'

STOOL: 'Story Ed. Yeah, I'm taking care of my mother. I honestly don't think she has much more time to live'.

ED: 'Ah, sorry to hear that mate. I've lost both my parents recently too. I'm still fairly numb as my dad passed away just over a year ago'.

STOOL: 'I know how you feel. My dad died a few years back aswell'.

ED: 'You have to tell yourself they are in a better place and happier than they have ever been otherwise you'd go insane, ey?'

STOOL: 'I agree. Thankfully I've a strong faith'.

ED: 'That's good to hear. I have also and it gives me great hope'.

STOOL: 'Good stuff pal. What has you in here, are you collecting a prescription or something?'

ED: 'I am. I'm not totally well myself'.

STOOL: 'What's wrong with you?'

ED: 'I wouldn't know where to start. I have everything. I'm taking so much medication I'd say the only thing I'm not 'on' at this stage is The Cross at Easter time'!

STOOL: 'Well, good ol' J.C. did bear it all so maybe you should pray over your illnesses, rebuke them and command them to leave in His Name'.

ED: 'I do that all the time, Stool but I have bitterness issues and that's why I'm not healing fully'.

STOOL: 'I understand, Ed. The Lord bore your sins too so if you don't forgive, you'll not be delivered. You should approach your enemies and make a reconciliation offer'.

ED: 'Yeah. It's tough to forgive fully but if the people who hurt me were to be humble enough to accept they were very cruel to me, I'd have no problem in letting the past go. Maybe I'm being paranoid but I've always had to forgive unconditionally. I can't do it anymore, they'll have to accept they were in the wrong'.

STOOL: 'I'd say you'd be the type to not bear grudges alright'.

ED: 'I've had my forgiving nature abused and taken for granted'.

STOOL: 'I'm sure they regret their attitude towards you'.

ED: 'I'd like to think so. We are all mature adults now so there's no point in being childish'.

STOOL: 'True. But don't be afraid to stand your ground either. If they abused your forgiving nature as you said, that's a miserable thing to do'.

ED: 'If they offered an apology, I'd try to forgive and forget alright'.

STOOL: 'Good man. Take good care of yourself'.

ED: 'Cheers buddy. See you soon'.

SCENE FROM A GOLF CLUBHOUSE—A FEW GUYS ARE HAVING A CONVERSATION.

VINCENT: 'That's a rather sizeable group on the first tee, ey?'

BAZ: 'It is, yeah. They don't look like they are Irish'.

TOMMY: 'Oh, one of the barmen told me last week they were expecting a crew from Sweden this weekend. It's probably them'.

VINCENT: 'Sweden has produced some top players over the last few decades. I wonder if they are any good'.

TOMMY: 'Apparently five of them are professionals'.

BAZ: 'This isn't a tough course at all. It probably won't be any sort of a challenge for them'.

VINCENT: 'They'll shoot well below par for sure and because they're Swedish, there'll be a whole load of 'hurdy birdies' ey?'!

TOMMY: 'That's not politically correct, Vincent'.

VINCENT: 'Listen, to enforce political correctness upon others is in itself politically incorrect as no one individual is the sole blessee of wisdom'!

BAZ: 'Good man, Vince. There's a lot to be said for aspects of existentialism and living and letting live although to furnish others with knowledge they may not possess is a good thing to do, ey?'!

TOMMY: 'So long as you are not being patronising. You have to respect people's intuition because, as Vincent revealed, we all have something to learn from one another'!

VINCENT: 'Ah here, this conversation is getting a bit serious. It's way too early for all of that'!

THE MEN AGREE AND FOCUS THEIR ATTENTION BACK ON THE FIRST TEE.

SCENE FROM A LIVING ROOM—BILL AND GAFFO ARE HAVING A CHAT.

BILL: 'There's a new family who've moved in across the road'.

GAFFO: 'How many of them are there?'

BILL: 'Six. The husband, wife and four young children'.

GAFFO: 'Have they introduced themselves yet?'

BILL: 'I just said hello to the lady this morning'.

GAFFO: 'Do you know where they're from?'

BILL: 'I believe they are from Marino (on Dublin's north side) originally'.

GAFFO: 'Have you any idea what their name is?'

BILL: 'Stones'.

GAFFO: 'I wonder if one of the kids is called 'People In Glass Houses Shouldn't Throw''!

BILL: 'Oh, right. 'People in glass houses shouldn't throw stones'. That's fairly witty, Gaffo but I tell ya people in glass houses shouldn't 'throw' orgies either otherwise their neighbours might see them and the word will spread what a pack of dirty feckers there are living in and visiting the locality'!

GAFFO: 'Goodness me, you're gas! Where did that come from? You're fairly witty too mate. Wait 'til I tell your new neighbours what you've just said'!

BILL: 'Oh no, please don't do that. I'll be mortified'.

GAFFO: 'Don't worry. I won't say a thing but even if I did, I'd say they've a sense of humour'!

SCENE FROM A PARK—A YOUNG COUPLE (EOGHAN AND TARA) ARE WALKING TOGETHER.

EOGHAN: 'Let's go over to the old pond, Tara?'

TARA: 'Okay. That'll be nice'.

EOGHAN: 'Look, there's Billy Keane's little sister, Aoife, with a young lad'.

TARA: 'Billy was telling me she was dating some boy from Baldoyle (on Dublin's north side). He's meant to be very bright'.

EOGHAN: 'Do you know his name?'

TARA: 'Ruairi Hiney'.

EOGHAN: 'Well, I hope he's nice to her or his first name will become 'Boot Up Your Little''!

TARA: 'Yeah, Billy would kick his ass alright if he hurt Aoife. He dotes on her'.

EOGHAN: 'I'm sure he's a nice young fella but I'd imagine Aoife would be able to take care of herself anyway'.

TARA: 'Mmm, she probably would. She's tough'.

THE COUPLE CONTINUE TO STROLL AROUND.

SCENE FROM A CRICKET PAVILLION—A GROUP OF MEN ARE WATCHING A GAME AND HAVING A FEW DRINKS.

DEV: 'This one's going down to the wire, ey?'

GEORGIE: 'It is but I'd say getting twenty one runs off the last two overs is possible'.

BUDGIE: 'Yeah, I'd say so too but we only have one wicket left. I don't think we are going to win this match'.

CUT TO A SCENE FROM THE CREASE. THE BOWLER DELIVERS THE BALL AND TAKES OUT OFF STUMP. THE GAME IS OVER.

CUT BACK TO THE SCENE IN THE PAVILLION. THE MEN ARE DISAPPOINTED.

BUDGIE: 'I fecking told you we'd lose that last wicket. Robin Smythe was the one guy I'd have hated to depend on to get the winning runs'.

DEV: 'You were proved right, Budgie'.

GEORGIE: 'Yeah. He only averages about ten runs per innings'.

BUDGIE: 'The fecking muppet. The bloke gets bowled so often, he makes brass look like it had just come out of confession'!

DEV: 'Bold as brass, ey? That was quite sharp on your behalf, Budge'!

THE CHAPS WALK BACK TO THEIR SEATS WITH SMILES ON THEIR FACES DESPITE BEING DISAPPOINTED WITH THE OUTCOME OF THE GAME.

SCENE FROM THE DART (Dublin Area Rapid Transit)—TWO FRIENDS (MICK AND LIAM) ARE HAVING A CHAT.

MICK: 'How many kids have you got now, Liam?'

LIAM: 'Three. Two girls and a boy who's the youngest'.

MICK: 'I suppose they are still in school, ey? My four are'.

LIAM: 'They are and are doing very well. However, I feel my boy is under-achieving. His teachers tell me he's extremely bright but he seems to be getting caught up in a bit of a 'lad culture''.

MICK: 'Yeah, that can happen to young fellas in their teens alright'.

LIAM: 'He's due to do his Junior Cert this year. I'm going to have to put my foot down a bit with him. He loves his laptop so much, I think he's neglecting his studies slightly'.

MICK: 'I understand. The internet can become addictive'.

LIAM: 'He's a great kid but the little b*llix is on the 'web' so often, you'd swear he was one of those blue-arsed flies with a death wish'!

MICK: 'Well, if he has his dad's sense of humour, he might become a stand-up comedian one day. You're fecking bonkers, Liamo'!

LIAM: 'Cheers Mick. I know you mean that in a good way mate'!

SCENE FROM A PARK—TWO MEN IN THEIR FIFTIES ARE WATCHING A GAME.

WILLIE: 'The number ten in black and white is a good little player, ey?'

PADDY: 'I was just thinking that to myself, Willie. He catches the eye'.

WILLIE: 'Here, Paddy. That's Niall O'Gorman across the way in the red waterproofs, isn't it?'

PADDY: 'I think it is alright. He's a coach with the Ireland U-16's. He's with Noel Berry. That w*nker is notorious for poaching players from other clubs'.

WILLIE: 'I know. Apparently he's called 'Yellow Jaundice' over in Glasnevin (on Dublin's north side)'.

PADDY: 'Why? Is he a gargler aswell or something?'

WILLIE: 'No, he's a tee-totaler but they nicknamed him it because he's forever 'on the tap' of another sort if you know what I mean'!

PADDY: 'Oh, right. Well, he better not try take our finest prospects or I'll stick this umbrella up his arse'!

WILLIE: 'C'mon, let's go over and warn Jimmy McDevitt he's about. His team are progressing well and he'd freak if he was to lose his best players now. He's invested a lot of his time developing them'.

SCENE FROM A NIGHT-CLUB—FERGAL AND SAOIRSE ARE A YOUNG COUPLE HAVING A DRINK BESIDE THE DANCE-FLOOR.

FERGAL: 'That guy in the blue jumper is a good dancer, ey?'

SAOIRSE: 'He is. His name is Stuart Delph. He's from Portmarnock (on Dublin's north side)'.

FERGAL: 'Oh, right. I recognise him now'.

SAOIRSE: 'He went to my friend, Sonia O'Grady's, debs. Do you not remember his tartan dickie bow?'

FERGAL: 'Ah, yeah. It's all coming back to me now'.

SAOIRSE: 'He's extremely intelligent. He's studying Medicine in Trinity College'.

FERGAL: 'Fair play to him but I heard his brother, Randy, is a gynaecologist and would even get up on the 'crack' in a saucer'!

SAOIRSE: 'Sweet Jesus, Ferg. You really do have some imagination'!

FERGAL: 'I'll take that as a compliment, Saoirse. C'mon, let's go out for a bit of a bop ourselves'.

SCENE FROM AN OFFICE—AINE AND JACQUI ARE SITTING AT THEIR DESKS.

AINE: 'I see Valuations took on a good-looking Dutch guy, Jacqui'.

JACQUI: 'Did they. Ooh. I must go over and see what he's like'.

AINE: 'He's meant to be really sweet too'.

JACQUI: 'Is he. What's his name?'

AINE: 'Roger De Laet'.

JACQUI: 'What part of The Netherlands is he from?'

AINE: 'Rotterdam'.

JACQUI: 'Wow. I'll go around now and try to check him out'.

AINE: 'Okay. He's really cute, try not to get too flustered'!

JACQUI: 'Oh, stop. Of course I won't'!

JACQUI GETS UP FROM HER SEAT TO GO TO THE OTHER SIDE OF THE BUILDING. SHE RETURNS.

AINE: 'Well, are you impressed'.

JACQUI: 'I asked around but he's not in yet'.

AINE: 'Hold on. You probably didn't look properly. I'll go around to locate him'.

AINE GETS UP AND VENTURES AROUND AND COMES BACK SEVERAL MINUTES LATER.

JACQUI: 'Is he there?'

AINE: 'He's there now'.

JACQUI: 'Great. What does he look like?'

AINE: 'He's tall, dark and handsome'!

JACQUI: 'I'm going around for another look'!

JACQUI GETS UP AGAIN AND RETURNS AFTER A FEW MINUTES.

AINE: 'Did you see him this time?'

JACQUI: 'I did. He's gorgeous. He was talking to Toni Devine. The bitch'!

AINE: 'That's his supervisor'.

JACQUI: 'Oh, he was explaining that he had missed his train and that's why he was not on time'.

AINE: 'Do you like his accent? It's sexy, ey? What was he saying to her exactly?'

JACQUI: 'To whom it concherns, dish ish De Laet's late show'!

THE TWO GIRLS CRACK UP AND GET UP TO GO TO THE CANTEEN IN THE HOPE ROGER WILL BE THERE.

SCENE FROM A SECONDARY SCHOOL CLASS-ROOM—A TEACHER IS GIVING A SEX EDUCATION LESSON.

TEACHER: 'Okay. Could you sum up sex in three words, Brian?'

BRIAN: 'How about 'Love. Touch. One-ness', sir?'

TEACHER: 'That's pretty good, Brian. Well done. How about you, Shane?'.

SHANE: 'I'll go for 'Intimacy. Sensuality. Orgasmic''.

TEACHER: 'Well done, Shane. What about you, Cormac?'

CORMAC: 'Erm, in my opinion it could be summed up as 'Computer. Charity. Surfing''!

THE WHOLE CLASS PLUS THE TEACHER GET VERY CONFUSED.

TEACHER: 'You're going to have to explain that to us all, Cormac. You have to appreciate we are rather puzzled'.

CORMAC: 'Well, when a straight couple have sex, it's like a computer because there's a 'log out'. When a couple of lesbians pleasure each other, it's like a charity because you get a 'hand out'. And when gay men have sex, it's like surfing because afterwards there's a 'wipe out'!

THE STUDENTS ERUPT INTO LAUGHTER AND EVEN THE TEACHER BEGINS TO CHUCKLE.

SCENE FROM A KITCHEN—A COUPLE OF BROTHERS (LASS AND SKINNO) ARE HAVING BREAKFAST.

LASS: 'You've lost a bit of weight, Skinno. Have you been on a diet?'

SKINNO: 'Yeah. I've a bit of work coming my way in about six weeks and I'm trying to lose a few pounds so I can get up and down on those ladders easily'.

LASS: 'Well, you're doing the right thing by having a good breakfast. It's very important you eat early in the day as it helps you to not pick on things later at night'.

SKINNO: 'I know how important breakfast is but even if I wasn't dieting, you still wouldn't catch me skipping it'.

LASS: 'Fair play to you'.

SKINNO: 'Too right. You're the same. Even if our breakfasts were 'the light fandango' covered in Marmite, they still wouldn't be skipped'!

LASS LAUGHS.

LASS: 'Go 'way out of that ya mad yoke'!

SCENE FROM A YOUTH CLUB—A LEADER IS CONDUCTING A SESSION WITH SOME KIDS.

LEADER: 'Okay lads. Do you know what you would like to get up to this week?'

ADAM: 'How about we play some games?'

LEADER: 'Yeah, that's a great idea, Adam. Could any of you suggest something in particular?'

CIAN: 'How about 'Hide 'n' Seek'?'

LEADER: 'Great stuff, Cian. Right. I'll count to fifty and then I'll try find you'.

THE LEADER TURNS HIS BACK, COVERS HIS FACE AND BEGINS TO COUNT OUT LOUD. WHEN HE FINISHES, HE GOES OFF TO FIND THE LADS. HOWEVER, HE HAS HARDLY EXITED THE CLUB WHEN HE SEES ONE OF THE BOYS TRADING BLOWS WITH AN OLDER TEENAGE GUY WHO APPEARS TO BE A FOREIGN NATIONAL. HE RUSHES OVER TO SPLIT THE TWO OF THEM UP.

LEADER: 'For goodness sake. Break it up lads'.

EVENTUALLY HE DRAGS THE IRISH LAD AWAY.

LEADER: 'What was that all about, Jacob?'

JACOB: 'Well, we were playing the game suggested so I grabbed the first bloke I saw in a turbin and gave him a few slaps'!

LEADER: 'What's that got to do with 'Hide 'n' Seek'?'

JACOB: 'Oh, I thought it was called 'Hidin' Sikh' so I believed it was all about giving some sikh a hiding, Leader'!

THE LEADER BREAKS OUT IN LAUGHTER AS DO ALL THE OTHER YOUTHS WHO HAVE GATHERED ROUND TO SEE WHAT WAS GOING ON!

SCENE FROM A NEWSPAPER OFFICE—MATT IS A NEW SOCCER CORRESPONDENT AND IS TALKING AWAY TO THE EDITOR (EVAN).

MATT: 'That match I was at last night wasn't great. It's going to be difficult doing a write-up about it'.

EVAN: 'Not much action in either penalty box, ey?'

MATT: 'You're right there wasn't. Only one goal scored by Sam Hall but he did go in goal after their 'keeper went off injured having used all of their substitutes'.

EVAN: 'Well, it's in these situations I'm sure you'll prove your worth to us, Matt'.

MATT GOES OFF AND TYPES UP HIS REPORT. HE E-MAILS IT TO EVAN AND HE IS PLEASED WITH ITS' WORDING. EVAN GOES BACK TO MATT AND ASKS HIM IF HE HAS ANY IDEAS ABOUT WHAT HEADLINE THEY SHOULD USE.

MATT RACKS HIS BRAIN TRYING TO THINK OF SOMETHING CATCHY. HE COMES UP WITH SOMETHING AND WALKS OVER TO EVAN TO SUGGEST IT.

MATT: 'I've come up with a headline, Evan'.

EVAN: 'Okay. What is it?'

MATT: 'How about 'The Three Musketeers''.

EVAN: 'For goodness sake. Where the feck are you coming from with that one?'

MATT: 'Well, because he scored the only goal and then went in goal, it could be a case of 'One For Hall And Hall For #1''!

EVAN: 'Go off out of that. That's far too cryptic you muppet'!

MATT RETURNS TO HIS DESK DISAPPOINTED HE'S FAILED TO IMPRESS HIS NEW BOSS.

SCENE FROM A LIVING ROOM—JON AND ANGEL ARE SITTING ON THE SOFA WATCHING A GAME OF SOCCER TOGETHER DURING EARLY APRIL.

JON: 'This match has started off at a blistering pace, Angel'.

ANGEL: 'The ball and players seem to be moving about very quickly alright, Jon'.

JON: 'Do you see that number seventeen in the sky blue?'

ANGEL: 'Oh, yeah. I just spotted him there now. Why?'

JON: 'He's a bit of a cheat. He's forever diving around looking for things off the ref. Most people don't like his play-acting'.

ANGEL: 'I'm sure his own fans aren't too bothered though, ey?'

JON: 'Yeah, you're right there I suppose. Look! The git's at it again'!

ANGEL: 'I see what you mean. Oh, the referee is going to his pocket'.

JON: 'Great. It's a yellow for him. I'm delighted'.

ANGEL BEGINS TO GIGGLE.

ANGEL: 'You don't like him, do you?'!

JON: 'No, I don't. If the Titanic was condemned to hell on Groundhog Day, it wouldn't go down as often'!

ANGEL CONTINUES TO CHUCKLE AWAY.

SCENE FROM A NEWSPAPER EDITOR'S OFFICE IN DUBLIN—
STEVE IS TRYING TO COME UP WITH A FOOTBALL HEADLINE
WITH MARK WHO'S A REPORTER.

STEVE: 'What score did the match end up as?'

MARK: 'Six nil to the Shannon Shamrocks'.

STEVE: 'Goodness me, that's some thrashing. Have you any interesting statistics?'

MARK: 'It was the manager of the Armagh Adders' one thousandth competitive game in charge'.

STEVE THINKS AWAY TO HIMSELF.

MARK: 'What are you pondering?'

STEVE: 'It's St. Patrick's Day today. I'm obviously trying to come up with an appropriate headline. Have you any suggestions?'

MARK: 'How about 'Romp-ee Pythons' given the beaten side's name, that it is held St. Patrick drove all the snakes out of Ireland and you're trying to be comical?'!

STEVE: 'Would you feck off out of that. Nobody would cop that'.

MARK: 'Well, how about 'Cead MILE Slaughtered' as it was the coach's one thousandth game, the fact that they were heavily defeated and with 'Mile' being the Gaelic for thousand?'!

STEVE SPLUTTERS.

STEVE: 'Very good, Mark. I think we'll go with that alright'.

SCENE FROM A TRAIN STATION—BOO HAS BUMPED INTO HIS
PAL SHEEPY.

BOO: 'Alright, Sheepy. I suppose you're on the way home
from work, ey?'

SHEEPY: 'I am. I started a new job with a solicitor there a
few weeks back. I take it you've just finished too?'

BOO: 'Yeah. Are you going to stop off in the gym to do a
work-out before going home?'

SHEEPY: 'That's fairly sharp on your behalf. You spotted my
sports bag and put two and two together, right?'

BOO: 'I did'.

THE TRAIN PULLS INTO THE STATION AND BOTH MEN GET ON.
SHEEPY SPOTS A GUY HE KNOWS AND SUGGESTS HE AND BOO GO
OVER TO CHAT TO HIM.

SHEEPY: 'Hi there, this is my friend Boo'.

SHEEPY'S FRIEND: 'Hello. Nice to meet you'.

BOO: 'You're not Irish, are you?'

SHEEPY'S FRIEND: 'No. I am from Honduras'.

BOO: 'That's cool. What's your name pal?'

SHEEPY'S FRIEND: 'Harold Palacios. I was called after that
famous British Prime Minister'.

BOO: 'Well, whatever about your first name, it
sounds like your surname is a Greek island I
got a great tan on last Summer mate'!

SHEEPY AND HAROLD START TO GIGGLE.

SCENE FROM A SEAFRONT—PIX AND DERMO ARE OUT ON A JOG.

PIX: 'It's great to see Spring coming in, ey?'

DERMO: 'Yeah. It's my favourite time of the year'.

PIX: 'The lengthening of the days really lifts one's spirits'.

DERMO: 'We're fairly north on the globe. We get dark winters but I'd hate to live in northern Finland or somewhere like that as they must get hardly any daylight in the depths of Winter'.

PIX: 'It must be a very black country during December and January alright'.

DERMO: 'I reckon it's even more of a 'black country' than when people from the English West Midlands dress up as minstrels in central Africa'!

PIX: 'Bahahaha. That's gas, Dermo'!

THE TWO GUYS CHUCKLE AWAY WHILE CONTINUING TO RUN.

SCENE FROM A CHIPPER IN BALLYFERMOT (ON DUBLIN'S SOUTH SIDE)—WES HAS BUMPED INTO HIS EX-GIRLFRIEND (JOANNE).

WES: 'Hi Joanne. How are you keeping?'

JOANNE: 'I'm grand thanks, Wes. And yourself?'

WES: 'I'm not too bad. Are you on your way home after a few drinks?'

JOANNE: 'I am. I'm a little bit tipsy'.

WES: 'Will you be alright getting home safely?'

JOANNE: 'Ah yeah, I will. My fella is outside'.

WES: 'Oh, you've met someone new. Who is he?'

JOANNE: 'He's from Lucan. I don't think you'd know him'.

WES: 'What's his name?'

JOANNE: 'El Burns'.

WES: 'I suppose that's what Spanish devil worshippers will feel when they're fecked in to the lake of fire, ey?'!

JOANNE: 'Aw, right. El burns. That's very witty on your behalf. You haven't lost your sense of humour anyway'!

WES: 'Cheers. Well, it was nice to bump into you again'.

THE COUPLE SAY GOODBYE AND WISH EACH OTHER THE BEST BEFORE WES EXITS THE TAKE-AWAY WITH HIS FOOD.

SCENE FROM A BEDROOM—A YOUNG COUPLE (CATHY AND JAMES) ARE CHATTING.

CATHY: 'Did you check out our mail box today yet, James?'

JAMES: 'No, I didn't. I take it you haven't taken it in either, ey?'

CATHY: 'Would you mind going down to see if there's anything there? I'm expecting an important document from my bank'.

JAMES: 'Yeah, no probs'.

JAMES LEAVES THE ROOM AND RETURNS SEVERAL MINUTES LATER WITH A FEW ENVELOPES.

JAMES: 'There you go, Cathy'.

CATHY: 'Cheers, James'.

JAMES: 'Is the letter from the bank there?'

CATHY: 'It's here alright. Oh, there's one for that new girl who just moved in next door. It was delivered here by mistake I'd imagine. The number on the address is for that house anyway'.

JAMES: 'Oh, I see. What's her name by the way?'

CATHY: 'It's addressed to a Miss Ann Somero'.

JAMES: 'Miss Ann Somero? For goodness sake, the person who sent her that letter must have thought he/she was posting it to a type of car'!

CATHY: 'What? Aw, Miss Ann Somero. I get it. You're gas, James'!

JAMES: 'Here. Give it to me and I'll drop it into her'.

CATHY HANDS JAMES THE LETTER AND HE LEAVES THE BEDROOM ONCE AGAIN.

SCENE FROM A RESTAURANT—CATHY AND JAMES HAVE GONE OUT FOR A MEAL.

CATHY: 'There's great variety on the menu, James, ey?'

JAMES: 'There is. I can't decide what I'd like to have'.

CATHY: 'Neither can I. I haven't had duck in a while'.

JAMES: 'Funny you should say that as that's precisely what I was just thinking'.

CATHY: 'Look, it's possible to get it Bombay or Peking style'.

JAMES: 'Yeah. Is there any other way you could have it?'

CATHY: 'Aromatic. Pity they don't do Dublin duck, it would give us something to be proud of, ey?'!

JAMES: 'Indeed. Although my local GP is a Dublin duck all of his own'!

CATHY: 'What do you mean?'

JAMES: 'Well, when I went to him last, he told me jokes while prescribing paracetamol for a skin infection so the bloke could be described as being 'great quack altogether', right?'!

SCENE FROM A HOUSE—A MARRIED COUPLE (JOSEPH AND SHARON) ARE HAVING A CHAT ABOUT THEIR HOME AFFAIRS.

JOSEPH: 'We need to do a bit of grocery shopping. The fridge and cupboards are getting a little bare'.

SHARON: 'Yeah. I'll write up a list of things tomorrow and you can go for them over the weekend'.

JOSEPH: 'Is there anything else that requires attention?'

SHARON: 'I did a whites wash today so yours, mine and the kids t-shirts will have to be ironed'.

JOSEPH: 'Ah, Sharon. You know how much I hate ironing, could you not do it?'

SHARON: 'No, I won't. I've ironed practically everything we've washed over the past fortnight'.

JOSEPH: 'You fecking wagon. You'll have me worn out'!

SHARON: 'Now, now, Joseph. It's not as if I give you so many chores, it's willy nilly'!

JOSEPH: 'Argh, I'm going to be knackered after all that. 'Girl You Know It's True''!

SHARON: 'Give over ya weakling. It should be no trouble to you'.

JOSEPH: 'As if. 'Baby, Don't You Lose My Number''!

SHARON: 'What at all are you on about you weirdo?'!

JOSEPH: 'What the feck am I on about? You're the one who started this whole 'Willy Nilly' cr*p'!

IT DAWNS ON SHARON WHAT JOSEPH IS MAKING REFERENCE TO.

SHARON: 'Bahahaha. You're bonkers'!

JOSEPH: 'Ha ha. I had you going for a bit, ey?'!

SHARON: 'Yeah, you did alright. That was pretty funny and if the t-shirts are still too wet to iron, you'll probably 'Blame It On The Rain', ey?'!

JOSEPH: 'Sweet Jesus. We're as fecking corny'!

SHARON: 'You're getting a taste of your own medicine'!

JOSEPH: 'Okay then. It was me who decided to turn 'willy nilly' into Milli Vanilli. Let's stop this conversation. I'll do the shopping and ironing. No probs love'!

SCENE FROM A SITTING ROOM—MIKE IS IN HIS LATE TEENS
AND HAS INVITED HIS MATES AROUND FOR A FEW CANS OF
BEER.

PAPPSY: 'Hey Mike. Siobhan Muldoon. Would you?'

MIKE: 'Yeah. I think I would she's pretty hot'.

CAMEL: 'Hey Dessie. Maria Doyle. Would you?'

DESSIE: 'I might. She'd be alright if she lost a bit of weight?'

MIKE: 'Hey Kavs. I know what you're going to say to this
            but Ita Brown-Windass. Would you?'

KAVS: 'I already have'.

THE LADS LET A COLLECTIVE GROAN OUT OF THEM.

PAPPSY: 'Aw, for feck sake. You must be even more
            desperate than an asexual nymphomaniac monk'!

DESSIE: 'When did you, Kavs?'

KAVS: 'When I was on vacation in South Africa'!

MIKE: 'Methinks you're acting the flute mate. You 'did' Ita
            Brown-Windass in South Africa?'!

KAVS: 'Yeah, I did eat a brown wind ass. I had the rump
            of an mpala with French fries and sauted onions in
            Durban but I don't know if it ate mushy peas before
            being snared'!

THE LADS ARE FED UP AT THE FACT THAT KAVS HAS DIGRESSED
AND BEGIN TO FIRE SOME OF THE FINGER FOOD AT HIM.

PAPPSY: 'Go off out of that you freak'!

DESSIE: 'And here was me thinking we'd all have had something to hold against you if were to sh*g someone unattractive ourselves you fecking smart-ass'!

KAVS: 'Well, I'm glad I caught you all out. It will teach you to be more respectful towards girls' appearances. They have feelings you know'!

MIKE: 'Don't be so deep, Kavs. I'm sure they poke fun at the way we look too! My attitude is that I'm young and can't be bothered with being serious'!

PAPPSY: 'Yeah, lighten up, Kavs. I just like big boobs and couldn't care too much about her face. You don't look at the mantelpiece when you are poking the fire'!

KAVS: 'I suppose you are all right. I actually do like a pretty face as you don't look at the screen when you are changing a disc in the dvd player but I bet you'd all prefer to see a flick of Miss World contestants putting on make-up than see a group of freckly, zit-ridden female Roma gypsies in werewolf masks pulling faces at a wicked witch of the west look-alike competition, ey?'!

DESSIE: 'Now you're adopting the proper attitude, Kavs. Plenty more times to be respectful when they desist from being bitchy themselves'!

KAVS: 'Cheers lads'.

SCENE FROM A TAXI—WHELO HAS PICKED UP A FARE AND IT
HAPPENS TO BE HIS MATE (DICEY).

WHELO: 'Story, Dicey. What's the craic with ya pal?'

DICEY: 'Howaya, Whelo. I'm great. How about you?'

WHELO: 'The recession has me by the goolies. Are you not struggling too?'

DICEY: 'No, I'm buoyant. You should watch a bit of The GOD Channel. His people thrive during downturns?'

WHELO: 'Is that right? Maybe it's the Lord I should be seeking alright'.

DICEY: 'You should give to charity or some ministry. You'll get it all back ten fold. When you give, it opens up avenues for God to do things for you and bless you financially'!

WHELO: 'Mmm. Listen, this conversation is getting a bit too deep for me but maybe I'll tune in some time tomorrow. How are your kids?'

DICEY: 'My ten year old son, Jack, has just taken up kick-boxing. He loves it'.

WHELO: 'Is he any good?'

DICEY: 'Yeah, he's brilliant. He has such a good right foot if he kicked snow off a rope at the North Pole, the snow would land at the South Pole with star dust embedded in it'!

WHELO: 'So the little fecker has great right swingers, ey?'

DICEY: 'Too right he has. You should see how he treats his opponents. If a mule was giving it to a female kangaroo doggy style, the duvet wouldn't be kicked and punched off as easily'!

WHELO: 'Bahahaha. The fecking little animal. Fair play to him'!

DICEY: 'He's a goer for sure. Hey Whelo, my gaff is the second left after the roundabout just in case I was distracting you'.

WHELO: 'No probs, Dicey. I'm used to talking while driving'.

WHELO PULLS THE CAB UP OUTSIDE DICEY'S HOUSE. DICEY GIVES WHELO TWENTY EURO FOR A TWELVE EURO FARE. THEY PROMISE EACH OTHER THEY'LL MEET UP FOR A PINT SOME TIME SOON. DICEY REMINDS WHELO NOT TO FORGET TO WATCH THE GOD CHANNEL BEFORE GETTING OUT. WHELO THANKS HIM AND BEEPS THE HORN AS HE DRIVES OFF.

SCENE FROM A COLLEGE BAR—PENNE SEES A GIRL (NIKKI) HE LIKES SO HE GOES OVER AND SITS DOWN BESIDE HER.

PENNE: 'Hi. How are ya?'

NIKKI: 'Oh, hi. I'm grand thanks. Who and how are you?'

PENNE: 'My name is Padraig but my mates called me Penne. I'm very well. Cheers for asking. What's your name?'

NIKKI: 'I'm Nikki. Why do your pals call you Penne?'

PENNE: 'I live in a house full of other students and when I go out for the groceries, the only pasta I ever buy is penne because it's my favourite type'!

NIKKI: 'That's pretty funny'!

ONE OF PENNE'S HOUSEMATES ENTERS THE BAR AND GOES OVER TO THE COUPLE.

MATE: 'Listen, the final installment of my allowance hasn't showed up in my account yet. Have you much money, Penne?'

PENNE: 'Here. There's twenty euro. I'm fairly stuck myself'.

MATE: 'Cheers buddy. That'll do for the moment. I'll give it back to you tomorrow. The funds should have shown up by then'.

PENNE'S MATE WALKS OFF UP TO THE BAR.

NIKKI: 'Much money, Penne? He must think you're that character who fancies 007 in the James Bond movies'!

PENNE: 'I don't know what you're on about, Nikki'.

NIKKI LOOKS AT PENNE AND IN A SCOTTISH ACCENT SAYS . . .

NIKKI: 'Mush Money Penne'!

PENNE CRACKS UP.

PENNE: 'Oh, right. I see where you are coming from. That's a first'!

THE YOUNG COUPLE CONTINUE TO FLIRT.

SCENE FROM A BUS IN DUBLIN—A COUPLE OF FRIENDS (CHARLIE AND EMMETT) ARE ON THEIR WAY INTO WORK.

CHARLIE: 'Alright, Emmett. How are you keeping mate?'

EMMETT: 'Ah, Charlie. I'm grand thanks. How about you?'

CHARLIE: 'I'm fine too. I presume you're on your way to work?'

EMMETT: 'I sure am. I suppose you are too, ey?'

CHARLIE: 'That's correct. You've lost a fair bit of weight'.

EMMETT: 'You're right. I've shed forty pounds over the last five months'.

CHARLIE: 'How did you manage that?'

EMMETT: 'Dieting, exercise and a lot of water consumption'.

CHARLIE: 'I thought you were going to tell me you took up a sport or something'.

EMMETT: 'Not at all. The playing of games involves putting oneself under unnecessary pressure to achieve completely inanimate outcomes'.

CHARLIE: 'Say what?'

EMMETT: 'You heard me. When Oscar Wilde said that playing a round of golf was a good walk spoiled, he was bang on'!

CHARLIE: 'Maybe but would practising the line-out in rugby not be a good way to prepare yourself for dusting off chandeliers in Georgian houses in the D2 area of this city, no?'!

EMMETT: 'Goodness me. Yeah, that could have its' benefits alright'!

THE MEN CONTINUE TO CHAT AWAY UNTIL THEIR DESTINATIONS HAVE BEEN REACHED.

SCENE FROM A UNIVERSITY—NIALL IS IN A POLITICS TUTORIAL.

TUTOR: 'Okay. Would any of you like to apply some political philosophy to how we could improve the world we live in?'

NIALL: 'Yes, I would. I'm fed up with how a few have power over the majority on the basis that they are stronger'!

TUTOR: 'Well, go on. Elaborate for us'.

NIALL: 'What I'm referring to is the secular world order'!

TUTOR: 'Explain what you mean, Niall'.

NIALL: 'What I mean is that finance is a necessary evil. The world has become increasingly materialistic and elitists have created a two-tiered society. We now have a secular world order whereby elitists are on top, their materialism below them (because they don't want to deal with it all themselves) and then the hard-working middle-class, working class and poor in general are beneath the materialism'!

TUTOR: 'Fair enough'.

NIALL: 'I'm not finished. When the Scriptures say 'all the strong shall be called weak and all the weak shall be called strong', I know what that means'!

TUTOR: 'Let us know what you feel this is in reference to'.

NIALL: 'The animalistic and those re-inforced by materialism shall be called weak. Those who are spiritual, not religiously inclined and are not feeding their materialistic egos will be called strong. In otherwords, power-players will be called weak and humble servants shall be called strong'!

TUTOR: 'That's very profound'.

NIALL: 'The materialistic secular world order is precisely that which will enable the son of perdition to crush spirits as Jesus Christ prophesised in the not-too-distant future. I'm telling yiz, things are rapidly closing in. I am a prophet and I sense it in my spirit. Materialism should be subject to spiritual laws, spirits should not be subject to materialistic lawlessness'!

TUTOR: 'This is excellent, Niall. Have you anything else to reveal to us?'

NIALL: 'I do. Some people are trying to suck us up into a power vacuum of materialistic ego-ness. They want to make out that we show regressiveness because we can't deal with obscene amounts of materialism but we are child-like whereas unwillingness to distribute wealth evenly is indicative of even greater regressiveness because it is child-ish. Feeding ones materialistic ego detracts from the individual's spirituality. It's very difficult to do the right thing when some have power over you when we are all equal'!

TUTOR: 'Tell us more'.

NIALL: 'We are meant to take dominion over the earth as God instructed us to but not subject it to worldliness. This whole notion that no one individual is bigger than the establishment is evil. The individuals that make up the establishments are not bigger than each other but they are than the establishment itself. As far as I'm concerned each spirit is worth more than an infinite amount of world economies. I'd like to think when I die I'll live on in the spirit realm for eternity. Establishments have life for sure, and are meant to, but in absolutely no way are they as valuable as the child of Yahweh. The service is meant to exist but to enhance the person's quality of life rather than be more important than it. Personal security and welfare is vital so that the worker is in a good state of health to perform the service and add to other human beings life quality although I accept the service contributes to more than just one person's quality of life'!

TUTOR: 'I see'.

NIALL: 'I'm telling yiz that if we allow God to be in control, He is not a Lord of condemnation but if we as little upstarts are in control, it is an offence against and in His Name as he takes it personally because nothing in this universe is outside the dominion of His rule and mind-frame. Power-players who want control over people are making others struggle while simultaneously taking the peaceful epic-ness out of life'!

TUTOR: 'Brilliant'.

NIALL: 'Thanks, tutor. When exam time comes around, I better get a fecking pass'!

TUTOR: 'I'm sure if you can come up with more wisdom like that, the person correcting your paper will be impressed and give you a very good grade'.

NIALL: 'I hope so'.

THE OTHER STUDENTS IN THE ROOM BEGIN TO APPLAUD NIALL.

SCENE FROM A BIBLE MEETING AT THE BEGINNING OF MARCH—DREW IS TALKING TO CORMAC.

DREW: 'Hi Cormac. Nice to have you back at the Bible fellowship once again'.

CORMAC: 'Cheers Drew. It's great to be here. What's on the agenda for tonight?'

DREW: 'We've an American chief Rabbi attending our meeting this evening'.

CORMAC: 'Excellent. I love Jewish people but we as Christians have been advised to provoke them to jealousy because we have Jesus. What's the Rabbi's name?'

DREW: 'He's called Benjamin Schamroth'.

CORMAC: 'Schamroth, ey? Does he know that the Irish Taoiseach gives a bowl of that stuff to the President of the United States on the White House lawn every St. Patrick's Day'!

DREW: 'Bahahaha. Well, I'm sure you can bring that up with him when he arrives. He'll probably see the funny side of it'!

SCENE FROM A STREET—SEAMIE HAS BUMPED INTO HIS NEIGHBOUR (CHRISTY).

SEAMIE: 'Alright Christy. How are you keeping mate?'

CHRISTY: 'Ah, not too bad thanks. Terrible bleedin' weather we've been having, ey?'

SEAMIE: 'I know. I got blown down the fecking road yesterday. Where are you off to now?'

CHRISTY: 'I'm going to visit my brother up in Beaumont Hospital. He was taken away by an ambulance last night. I think he has pneumonia'.

SEAMIE: 'More bad news. This is awful'.

CHRISTY: 'I'm only coming from a funeral too'.

SEAMIE: 'Aw, good night. Who's was it?'

CHRISTY: 'Jimmy 'Pigeon' Pouter's'.

SEAMIE: 'Are you serious? I worked with him down the docks. I didn't know he wasn't well. Nobody told me he had passed. I probably would have rambled down had I know it was taking place. What priest did the funeral?'

CHRISTY: 'Fr. Koumas. He's only new to the parish'.

SEAMIE GOES INTO A FIT.

CHRISTY: 'What on earth are you laughing at?'

SEAMIE: 'Just think about what you've just said'!

CHRISTY: 'Jimmy 'Pigeon' Pouter's funeral was done by Fr. Koumas. What's so fecking funny about that?'

SEAMIE IS STILL CHUCKLING AWAY BUT EVENTUALLY GATHERS HIMSELF.

SEAMIE: 'Do you not get it? Pigeon Pouter's funeral conducted by Fr. COO MASS'!

FINALLY IT REGISTERS WITH CHRISTY WHAT THE JOKE IS. HE BURSTS OUT.

CHRISTY: 'Wait and I tell the missus that one'!

THE TWO MEN CONTINUE TO GIGGLE BEFORE FINISHING OFF THEIR CONVERSATION.

SCENE FROM A LIVING ROOM—CATHY AND JAMES ARE
WATCHING A NEWS CHANNEL.

CATHY: 'How's that cup of tea, James?'

JAMES: 'Grand thanks, Cathy. There's just
                           about the right amount of milk in it.
                           Cheers'.

VOICE FROM THE TELLY: 'Thousands have gathered at an ultra-
                           Orthodox rally in Jerusalem today'.

JAMES: 'I love Jewish people. They really are
                           a blessed nation'.

CATHY: 'I know. If you have regard for
                           God's People, you will be judged
                           favourably'.

JAMES: 'Hey ultra-Orthodox? They recorded
                           the classic tunes 'Vienna' and
                           'Dancing With Tears In My Eyes', didn't
                           they?'!

CATHY BURSTS OUT GIGGLING.

CATHY: 'I'd tell you 'this means nothing to me' except for
           the fact you can probably see my eyes are watering.
           You're a fecking character and a half, James'!

JAMES: 'Nice to see you're on my wavelength once again
           baby'!

SCENE FROM A LIVING ROOM—TWO MEN (SEAMUS AND CORMAC) ARE WATCHING A SPORTS NEWS CHANNEL.

VOICE FROM THE TELLY: 'The funeral has taken place of ex-professional footballer Albert Lawson today'.

SEAMUS: 'Albert Lawson? I didn't know he had passed'.

CORMAC: 'Yeah, he died about two weeks ago'.

SEAMUS: 'Two weeks ago'?

CORMAC: 'Yep. He was ninety three'.

SEAMUS: 'It's not so much his age but the fact that it has taken so long for his funeral Mass to happen'.

CORMAC: 'That's the way they do things in the U.K. a lot of the time'.

SEAMUS: 'I'd find that traumatic if I was one of his children. I mean, if my dad died, I wouldn't want to be waiting around for a fortnight to bury him. I'd like to have it done within a few days'.

CORMAC: 'I know. The English have a strange tradition in that respect. If it took them as long to 'bury' a football in the back of the net as quickly as it takes them to 'bury' their loved ones, they'd never score a single goal let alone qualify for major tournaments, ey?'!

SEAMUS STARTS CHUCKLING.

SEAMUS: 'This is a very sombre moment. I really shouldn't be laughing at you'.

CORMAC: 'Would you go off out of that. They do nothing but laugh in Heaven. I know the Lord and, trust me, He is hysterical'!

SEAMUS: 'Okay, Cormac. Whatever you say. Maybe people should lighten up in scenarios like this alright'!

SCENE FROM A HOUSE—A GROUP OF THREE LADS IN THEIR LATE TEENS ARE HOLDING AN AUDITION TO RECRUIT A NEW BASS GUITAR PLAYER FOR THEIR BAND.

BONGO: 'When are we to expect the next candidate lads?'

REDSER: 'He said he'd be hear about half seven'.

SOAPIE: 'He's coming all the way from Rathfarnham (on Dublin's south side) so we're going to have to give him some leeway as he might get caught up in traffic'.

BONGO: 'Hold on. There's someone pulling up in a car outside. I'll check if it's him'.

BONGO EXITS THE GARAGE AND RETURNS WITH THE AUDITIONIST A COUPLE OF MINUTES LATER.

BONGO: 'Hey lads, this is Joshua Ndlovu'.

REDSER AND SOAPIE GET OFF THEIR SEATS, GO OVER, INTRODUCE THEMSELVES AND SHAKE JOSHUA'S HAND.

JOSHUA TAKES HIS BASS GUITAR OUT OF THE CASE, PLUGS IT INTO THE AMPLIFIER AND STARTS STRUMMING.

REDSER: 'By the way, where are you from originally mate?'

JOSHUA: 'I'm Irish but my dad is from Zimbabwe'.

SOAPIE: 'Woh, that's cool. Who are your influences?'

JOSHUA: 'I suppose Level 42 as I'm a big fan of funky Eighties music'.

BONGO: 'So, your name is Joshua Ndlovu and you're influenced by Level 42, ey? If we accept you into the band, do you mind if we nickname you 'Lessons'?'!

ALL FOUR LADS BREAK OUT IN LAUGHTER.

SCENE FROM A NEWS CHANNEL EDITING ROOM—SIMON (THE EDITOR) HAS A STORYLINE PUT TOGETHER AND IS LOOKING FOR A HEADLINE.

SIMON: 'Hey Katie. We've a really interesting breaking story here'.

KATIE: 'What is it?'

SIMON: 'A man in his forties was out on an inflatable, fell asleep, drifted off and had to be rescued'.

KATIE: 'Whereabouts?'

SIMON: 'Just off Lincolnshire on the English east coast'.

KATIE: 'Do you know anything about him?'

SIMON: 'Apparently he's a practising psychotherapist'.

KATIE: 'Oh, right. I suppose you're looking for something catchy to get the viewers' attention, ey?'

SIMON: 'Our reporters are on the ground but, you're right, I'm looking for a headline'.

KATIE: 'How about 'Shrink's In The Wash''!

SIMON CHUCKLES AND IS WELL IMPRESSED BY KATIE'S SUGGESTION.

SCENE FROM A PUB—SHAY AND HIS WIFE (BUBBLES) ARE HAVING A DRINK.

SHAY: 'I love finishing early of a Frydeh and going to de pub when it's empty, Bubbles'. (I love finishing early on Friday and going to the pub when it's empty, Bubbles).

BUBBLES: 'Yeah, oi enjoy me few drinks jurdin de day when yiv dun yaw week's wuhk too love'. (Yeah, I enjoy my few drinks during the day when you've done your week's work too love).

SHAY: 'Look. Heeaw comes Patch O'Toole. He's always in heeaw'. (Look. Here comes Patch O'Toole. He's always in here).

BUBBLES: 'Whah dih yeh meein hee duzz be always in heeaw? Duzz he naw have a job?' (What do you mean he does be in here? Does he not have a job?).

SHAY: 'No, he duzzin. He's a feckin' layzee so-and-so'. (No, he doesn't. He's a fecking lazy so-and-so).

BUBBLES: 'His wife must be well p*ssed off wirrim if he duzzin wuhk and gowiz on de beeaw all of de tyim'. (His wife must be well p*ssed off with him if he doesn't work and goes on the beer all of the time).

SHAY: 'I dohne know why she puts up wirrim. She duzz evreeting. She brings aw kids tih skooill den wuhks as eh part-tyim French polishaw'. (I don't know why she puts up with him. She does everything. She brings her kids to school then works as a part-time French polisher).

BUBBLES: 'Well, he cerh inlee izzin O'Tooill by nayim, O'Tooill by naychaw. I'd say dee owenlee tyim he's evvaw

51

lifted a tooill is when hee washizz his ballix in de showaw if hee even duzz dah much de duhty bahstud'! (Well, he certainly isn't O'Toole by name, O'Toole by nature. I'd say the only time he's ever lifted a tool is when he washes his scrotum in the shower if he even does that much the dirty b*stard!).

SHAY: I know. Poor Jill. The bloke duzz jack sh*t'. (I know. Poor Jill. The bloke does jack sh*t).

BUBBLES: 'Her nayim is Jill, ey? Funny dah. You could call dim Jack Sh*t & Jill-Of-All-Trayidz, ryh?'! (Her name is Jill, ey? Funny that. You could call them Jack Sh*t & Jill-Of-All-Trades, right?'!).

SHAY: 'Yeah, dats a good nayim to give the payaw alryh'! (Yeah, that's a good name to give the pair alright!).

SCENE FROM A WORKING CLASS HOUSE DURING THE EARLY EIGHTIES—SOME YOUNG LADS IN THEIR MID-TEENS ARE HEADING INTO TOWN TO TRY GET SERVED ALCOHOL.

WOBBLE COMES DOWN THE STAIRS FROM HIS BEDROOM AND ENTERS THE SITTING ROOM WHERE HIS FRIENDS ARE.

WOBBLE: 'Alright. Are we ready to head now lads?'

PELO: 'We are. You were up there a while. We've been waiting for the last twenty minutes. Woh, your moustache looks cool. It didn't look like that earlier today'.

GUNTER: 'Yeah, you'll easily pass for eighteen now, Wobble. How come it looks as thick as it is?'

WOBBLE: 'I put a bit of black boot polish through it'!

THE LADS LEAVE THE HOUSE AND ARE ON THEIR WAY INTO THE CITY ON A BUS.

PELO: 'I tell yiz what, we'll get Wobble to order the drinks as he's the one who looks the oldest with his moustache'.

GUNTER: 'That's a deadly idea'.

WOBBLE: 'I've no problem with that fellas'.

THE BUS ARRIVES AT ITS' DESTINATION AND THE YOUTHS GET OFF. THEY ENTER THE BOOZER. PELO AND GUNTER FIND AN ALCOVE WHILE WOBBLE GOES UP TO THE BAR.

THE BARMAN SEES WOBBLE AND GOES TO SERVE HIM BUT IS LOOKING AT HIM SUSPECTING HE MIGHT BE UNDERAGE.

BARMAN: 'Can I help you?'

WOBBLE: 'Give us three pints of lager please'.

BARMAN: 'What age are you?'

WOBBLE: 'I'm eighteen'.

BARMAN: 'You're not eighteen kiddo'.

WOBBLE: 'Of course I am'.

BARMAN: 'You look about fifteen to me'.

WOBBLE: 'Do you think a fifteen year old could grow a moustache like this?'!

BARMAN: 'That's a moustache?'

WOBBLE: 'What did you think it was buddy?'

BARMAN: 'Listen sunshine, come back to me in three years and I'll happily serve you alcohol. To be honest, I thought you'd rubbed beneath your nose after doing a newspaper delivery'!

WOBBLE: 'Stick it up your h*le mate'!

BARMAN: 'Go on, get out'.

WOBBLE GOES OVER TO HIS PALS AND TELLS THEM THE BARMAN WON'T SERVE HIM. THEY LEAVE THE PUB DISAPPOINTED AND TRY TO FIND ANOTHER BOOZER THAT WILL WELCOME THEM.

SCENE FROM A HOUSE—TWO GUYS (BRIAN AND ROBBIE) ARE HAVING A CHAT.

BRIAN: 'Hey, Robbie. What is homosexuality?'

ROBBIE: 'It's when a person of a particular gender is sexually attracted to someone of the same sex'.

BRIAN: 'I know that ya muppet. But what is it? You know what I mean'.

ROBBIE: 'I think it's a disorder of some sort'.

BRIAN: 'You told me you have a disorder too so does that not mean you are gay aswell, no?'

ROBBIE: 'I'm not. It's a bit like economics in that all Giffen goods are inferior goods but not all inferior goods are Giffen goods'!

BRIAN: 'You're going to have to explain that mate?'

ROBBIE: 'Do you not cop what I'm getting at? What I'm trying to say is that everyone who is homosexual has a disorder but not everybody who has a disorder is homosexual'.

BRIAN: 'Oh, right. I see where you are coming from although you have to respect you lost me with the reference to economics'.

ROBBIE: 'I understand. The master's degree I got in economic science has come in handy in more ways than one, ey?'!

BRIAN: 'It has but if two men fancy one another, is it not a case them possessing the female sexuality'?

ROBBIE: 'Of course not. Gay men are very much men. I told you, it's something to do with a disorder'.

BRIAN: 'Yeah, but if a man fancies a man, they have the female sexuality, are in actual fact females in this respect and because it's a case of femininity wanting to get it on with femininity should mean that gay men are called 'lesbians''!

ROBBIE: 'Aw, for goodness sake. I don't even know where to start with that. Listen, as far as I'm concerned it's whatever mind-set and disposition that is compatible with yours which determines your true sexual orientation regardless of whether you're male or female. Now shut up ya fecking gobsheen'!

SCENE FROM A BIBLE MEETING—A GROUP OF CHRISTIANS HAVE GATHERED TO READ SOME SCRIPTURE PASSAGES AND SING A FEW HYMNS.

CHAD: 'Do any of you have a favourite song of worship?'

DREW: 'Yeah, I love 'How Great Is Our God''.

CHAD: 'That's one that really stirs up my faith too, Drew. Well done'.

FRANK: 'One that gets me going is 'Yahweh Is The God Of My Redemption''.

CHAD: 'Another great choice, Frank. Maybe we can sing that one later aswell'.

CORMAC: 'I really like 'Lord, I Lift Your Name On High''.

CHAD: 'Yeah, we really should exalt the Name of Jesus, Cormac. It happens to be one of my favourites also'.

CORMAC: 'Indeed. I've actually written an additional verse of it myself'.

CHAD: 'Have you brother? Well, give us a small rendition of your composition and we'll try to join in'.

CORMAC GRABS A GUITAR AND BEGINS TO STRUM AWAY.

CORMAC (Singing): 'Lord, Your Second Coming's nigh. Lord, Your awesomeness amazes. Life really should mean life. Scumbags shouldn't call You Jayziz'!

THE GROUP ALL LOOK AT EACH OTHER IN EXASPERATION THEN BREAK OUT LAUGHING.

CHAD: 'Well, luckily the God we all know has a great sense of humour, Cormac'!

CORMAC: 'Ah, sure don't I know that'!

THE GROUP CONTINUE TO GIGGLE.

SCENE FROM A PUB IN GLASGOW—TWO PALS (KENNY AND HAMISH) HAVE ARRANGED TO MEET FOR SOME PINTS.

KENNY: 'Hiya dooin, Hamish?' (How are you doing, Hamish?).

HAMISH: 'Oh, am no too bad ya wee bashtad'! (Oh, I'm not too bad ya wee b*stard!).

KENNY: 'Am no a wee bashtad ya wee bashtad. Greeayh tee see ya pal'! (I'm not a wee b*stard ya wee b*stard. Great to see ya pal!).

HAMISH: 'Whaw argh ya drrrinkin'? (What are ya drinking?).

KENNY: 'I diznee nay whaw it's called, jost the local pish a thenk it idge'! (I don't know what it's called, just the local p*ss I think it is!).

HAMISH: 'Wewill, dee ya wawhin' anuthah pynh of et pal'! (Well, do ya want another pint of it pal!).

KENNY: 'Shoor. Why nawh?' (Sure. Why not?).

HAMISH GOES TO THE BAR AND ORDERS THE DRINKS. HE RETURNS WITH THEM.

HAMISH: 'Thereah yih goh, Kenneh'! (There you go, Kenny!).

KENNY: 'Cheearghs ya wee bashtad'! (Cheers ya wee b*stard!).

HAMISH: 'Soh, hoo have yih been keepain?!' (So, how have you been keeping?!).

KENNY: 'Nawthin' streeange aw wandahfoll. Am a bah doon as the Reign Josh ah no dooin' too wewill'! (Nothing strange or wonderful. I'm a bit down as the Rangers are not doing too well!).

HAMISH: 'Aye, wor strogglin' sense we losht ooargh bist playawdge. Ooargh coach ez haven moorah then a feeooh wee problams'! (Aye, we are struggling since we lost our best players. Our coach is having more than a few wee problems!).

KENNY: 'Eff that's no bad enoff ooargh top gool scorargh has been seedlined for sex months weeh a creeooshit knee legament anjooreh. He has a beh ov a wee problam too, ey?'! (If that's not bad enough our top goal scorer has been sidelined for six months with a cruciate knee ligament injury. He has a bit of a wee problem too, ey?!).

HAMISH: 'Aye, ah noo. Eff wee encoontar annee moorah 'wee' problams, the Cewilltech fans will beganne tee thenk we have feckin' prawsteet cansargh'! (Aye, I know. If we encounter any more 'wee' problems, the Celtic fans will begin to think we have feckin' prostate cancer!).

KENNY: 'Har har. That's pretteh funneh ya wee bashtad. Geh that pynh entee ya'! (Har har. That's pretty funny ya wee b*stard. Get that pint into ya!).

THE MEN CONTINUE TO CHAT AWAY.

SCENE FROM A STREET—TONY HAS BUMPED INTO HIS
NEIGHBOUR (DAR DAR) AND IS EAGER TO TALK TO HIM.

TONY: 'Alright, Dar Dar. How are things mate?'!

DAR DAR: 'Story, Tony. I know by the way you're looking you
            were talking to that bloke who lives on his own in
            the corner house and says he's the Counsellor again,
            weren't you?'!

TONY: 'You're right. You won't believe some of the stuff he
            was coming out with. I decided to take some notes'!

DAR DAR: 'Go on, let me have it. I'm intrigued by this guy'!

TONY: 'He's saying Jesus prophesised in the Gospel of John
            that 'the world cannot accept him for it neither
            knows him nor sees him. But you know him for
            he lives with you and in you. I will not leave you
            as orphans, I will come to you'. He said what he
            professed about being the Light of the World was
            a slight misinterpretation by him. The Church is
            the Light of the World but when Jesus revealed 'a
            town that is set in a hill cannot be hidden' he was
            definitely referring to Sutton and Howth (on Dublin's
            north side) and he is certainly the Spirit which is
            signified by the Lamp allusion. He continued that
            it's possibly his Lamp that shines through the
            Church'!

DAR DAR: 'Oh, I see'!

TONY: 'He made more references to Jesus Christ's Sermon
            on the Mount. He's maintaining He revealed the
            Beatitudes and then went off in a tangent and might
            have used the word 'Blessed' in a different way.
            He's saying the Lord knew that he would have a
            great sense of humour and a lot of it would include

going off in tangents and using double entendres. He says a minister on The GOD Channel referred to '2012 hysteria because of God's refiner's fire and fuller's soap' prior to 2012 and that one of his works that was published during 2012 could be 'The Little Book' which was foretold would 'have their stomachs churning' and is a book that Yahweh reveres'!

DAR DAR: 'What did Jesus say?'!

TONY: 'He asserts Christ prophesised 'and Blessed are you when people insult you, persecute you and falsely say all kinds of evil against you because of me. Rejoice and be glad, because great is your reward in heaven, for in the same way they persecuted the prophets who were before you''!

DAR DAR: 'Does that not relate to all Christians who have problems, no?'!

TONY: 'He said the Beatitude which came immediately before that goes as follows: 'Blessed are those who are persecuted because of righteousness'. According to him that could relate to followers of Christ. What he believes is that in the same way Yahweh and Yeshua are Blessed, so too is he as the Spirit, like what I told you the last time we spoke. He says that not every person who has problems, and is a Christian, is a prophet but he told me he is and that if one refers to The Creed they will know that 'he has spoken through the prophets' before he came to planet earth which Jesus was aware of. Although he asserts it could possibly be about all Christians alright but it's definitely something he can take personally too because of his experiences. He believes he is more persecuted than most because he's been treated badly by people who profess to be Christian themselves and that's the difference as far as he's concerned'!

DAR DAR: 'Did he tell you about any of the problems he has had because of his faith in Jesus and because of who he is?'!

TONY: 'He just said he got all kinds of hassle and he wasn't even allowed to be himself or stick up for himself and, while he was upset at his mistreatment, not even entitled to his emotions. He says he was driven to the brink of taking his own life he was so confused'!

DAR DAR: 'That's blooming terrible'!

TONY: 'He informed me that it was difficult for him to function. He said he felt like he was being totally violated and dictated to. He also revealed that another cruel thing is that (because of the day he was born on) he has eccentric traits and (because of the oppression and repression) his behaviour was becoming increasingly erratic'!

DAR DAR: 'Is there no wonder he was making mistakes, ey?'!

TONY: 'However, he accepts that people are going to deal with you if they feel like you are empowering yourself but these people and the treatment he had been, was and always knew he would get from the media was inducing him into making mistakes. His opinion is you shouldn't be the kind to exact retribution and that's why he made mistakes as he felt like he was being dictated to. His opinion is that Jesus Christ prophesised this and he's fairly sure He is on his side because he is His Father's Spirit afterall'!

DAR DAR: 'Yeah, I understand'!

TONY: 'He accepts he transgressed on occasions but when people continually feel the need to make you responsible when you want to take responsibility for your actions was frustrating for him. All he's ever wanted is the benefit of the doubt because he'd like to think he's a considerate individual'!

DAR DAR: 'He has to feel trusted, doesn't he?'!

TONY: 'He does alright'!

DAR DAR: 'It seems to me like everything has been very cruel on him. Maybe what Jesus said about the world not being able to accept him is true. If he is the Counsellor, we have to respect he evidences the high standards Yahweh has'!

TONY: 'He confessed that he has made mistakes himself, he has gone to confession regarding his transgressions and thinks maybe his persecutors should too as it would liberate them. But given who it is he is, it's a serious issue that he was driven to the brink of suicide'!

DAR DAR: 'He's the Spirit and has still gone to confession despite the fact he's equal with God and Jesus. That's very humble on his behalf'!

TONY: 'He says he forgives those who persecuted him and it's just a little unfortunate because he professes that he has been very misunderstood but they would have to accept that they did almost induce him into ending his own life. They just didn't know who it was they were dealing with and what his circumstances regarding the media had always been, ey?'!

DAR DAR: 'Yeah. Sounds to me like it's a very serious issue alright though'!

TONY: 'There was a direct reference made to what happened to him on a programme called 'Extreme Prophetic' on The GOD Channel by a guest minister several years ago according to him. He reflected that when it was becoming apparent to the man what his circumstances were, he almost broke down in tears when it was being revealed to him what he was going and put through by people'!

DAR DAR: 'That's powerful mate'!

TONY: 'He revealed that he wasn't able to get the necessary communication and closure from a friendship which has made it difficult for him to move on and meet someone new. Biological issues and the extreme guilt he felt he'd suffer from if he fornicated discouraged him from wanting to get involved with that someone special in addition. He cracked a joke by saying the girl he felt for (who had moved on) was the only female capable of making and keeping him 'perpendicular of body' as he put it! He has really struggled with his mental health welfare over the last twenty years too and that had disenabled him from entering a partnership aswell. He told me that during the Summer of 1992 he had asked Yahweh for his one hundred per cent pure spiritual love because he was frightened of having sex with a girl for just out of lust. He revealed with all the problems he had had with the media, he was side-tracked and de-secured from realising he is His Spirit! He said the only way he wanted to sleep with a girl was within the realms of a totally-loving and committed relationship. He says he's an ultra-sensitive individual'!

DAR DAR: 'Ah, he obviously is, Tony'!

TONY: 'He believes that the really sad thing for him is that when he confronts the son of perdition, he'll probably be aware of what has hurt him throughout his life and re-open his wounds. He thinks he'll probably act out the way the people who mistreated him's behaviour was towards him particularly that which broke his heart and drove him to the brink of suicide during his adult life. He's upset because he's known since his infancy that his life would always be destined towards extreme unhappiness. He's feeling at least some of his future is going to be very painful and that's a really frustrating and difficult thing for him to deal with'!

DAR DAR: 'Aw, Lord. This is very sad'!

TONY: 'He's harbouring the belief that it was all part of the media people conspiring against him during this time that he be taken out of the equation because, as I also told you the last time we talked, he revealed that Lucifer wants to be exalted and worshipped as God and planet earth is the only dominion in the universe where he can be. He says 'the beast' is going to demand he be worshipped. He continued that he can't help but get the impression that the evil media men were fuelling peoples' negative opinions of and attitudes towards him'!

DAR DAR: 'Yeah. I remember you telling me that the other day'!

TONY: 'He says the age of the 'son of perdition' is almost upon us'!

DAR DAR: 'There's a lot of people who are thinking that way. What did he have to say about this dictator?'!

TONY: 'He said it's all about rejecting many of the traditions of our forefathers as the Lord Jesus Christ advised. He told me when 'the beast' comes on the scene, he's going to try establish a one world system based on these empty traditions and will be religiously inclined in terms of them'!

DAR DAR: 'What traditions did he refer to?'!

TONY: 'Firstly, he told me that practically all the doctrines of the world's religions are non-sense. It's not about having a religion but an intimate relationship with The Almighty and His Son instead'!

DAR DAR: 'Tell me more'!

TONY: 'He admitted he didn't know too much about the world's religious doctrines (and didn't really want to) but just decided to reveal some things to me. For example, Muslims regard themselves as mono-theists because they believe GOD is the un-begotten who begets not. He said he accepts Yahweh is un-begotten but what he also knows is that He begets as Jesus Christ resided on earth at some stage and it was foretold in the Bible'!

DAR DAR: 'This is getting very deep but go on'!

TONY: 'Apparently Mohammed was shown a vision of Judgement Day and in it he is said to have seen GOD deny the fact that He had a Son. He honestly harbours the belief that this was The Almighty being sarcastic as why would He want to be securing to those who spent their whole lives rejecting and insulting Jesus Christ and not acknowledging the sacrifice He made for their sins and for the whole of mankind in general. He said what confuses him is that if Muslims are mono-theists then why do they say Mohammed is The Spirit? What he was getting at is if Mohammed now resides in Heaven as The Spirit, as they believe, then there must be at least two persons in The GOD Head i.e. Allah (which is what they call Him) and The Holy Spirit (GOD The Spirit). He continued that we, as believers in Jesus Christ, are 100% correct to understand that there are three persons in The GOD Head i.e. GOD The Father (Yahweh), GOD The Son (Jesus Christ) and The Lamp (i.e. which is what J.C. referred to in His Sermon on the Mount and signifies The Spirit—GOD The Spirit). As I told you the last time I met you he claims that he is the Counsellor who is currently residing here on planet earth and will go off to Heaven in a blaze of glory along with the other Witness (who is a Lamp of a different sort) as documented in the Book Of Revelations some time in the near future'!

DAR DAR: 'This is all very interesting. Go on, let me know more'!

TONY: 'He went on that some Muslims believe Mohammed ascended into Heaven from the streets of Jerusalem but it wasn't three and a half days after being martyred at the hands of the son of perdition (because he hasn't come on the scene yet) as what is written in this part of Scripture'!

DAR DAR: 'This is very thought-provoking. Continue'!

TONY: 'He enlightened me that accepting when Jesus Christ was crucified (and in-so-doing bore the sins of mankind) and rose three days later is the only way to salvation and when you know the truth, it sets you free which sees to it you are neither GOD-less nor religiously inclined. He quoted Scripture by saying 'it is for freedom that Christ has set us free'. He believes being part of an organised religion is a type of bondage and if we take the Body of Christ as a literal body, we will see that it has different parts with specific functions which are meant to act inter-dependently. This is where he says the various religious doctrines are flawed because if a child was born a knee cap and his dad an elbow joint, then how can the dad's elbow joint-ness dictate to the son's knee cap-ness which is by and large what organised religions, doctrines and so on do. In his opinion they distort that part's true function and uniqueness and prevent it from fulfilling itself. It's among the reasons why Christ advised us not to abide by the traditions of our fathers although dad's are meant to discipline their children and train them in righteousness but only if they know the truth themselves and haven't been dictated to by a different part of the Body Of Christ which may have had another specific function, unique personality etc who may have been indoctrinated. However, he respects that fathers have their intuition'!

DAR DAR: 'That's all news to me, Tony'!

TONY: 'He told me that both Jesus Christ and Mohammed knew he would exist at some stage in the future and what they revealed to those around them and passed down throughout the generations was about what would go on in his life and has possibly been incorporated into people's religious doctrines'!

DAR DAR: 'Well, I believe in Jesus Christ but you have to be careful when you are passing comments about another person's religious beliefs. People can get very offended as nobody likes the idea of not representing God properly. The fact that people get so upset is proof of the reality that He exists. What else did he have to say?'!

TONY: He says the son of perdition is going to proponentise peace and prosperity but he related to the Sermon on the Mount once again and reflected that the Lord warned about the dangers of loving money. He continued that if you feed your materialistic ego, you are damaging your own spirituality. He's certain Jesus made reference to how excessive materialism would damage His Father's Spirit and how the materially self-sufficient would treat the Counsellor'!

DAR DAR: 'This is all very interesting'!

TONY: 'He thinks being materially-inclined detracts from one's sexiness regardless of your gender. He believes Yahweh doesn't begrudge us our material possessions but it's as if the explosion of the world economy financially is generating too great an accessory attached to the object i.e. the price of it'!

DAR DAR: 'I'm sure he had more to tell you as this bloke seems to possess a lot of wisdom and knowledge'!

TONY: 'Yeah, he does alright. He enlightened me that 'the beast' will be a politician. He says seat number six hundred and sixty six is currently vacant in the European parliament but isn't going to remain so for much longer. He says Christ saw the religious and political arenas as one, He was correct to do so and that when Yahweh raises him up to be one of His witnesses, he will be subjecting the political scene to his fundamental beliefs. He thinks that party politics has become dictated to by finance and that financial people and politicians should be more influenced by the Bible as financial lawlessness dictating everything is inducing party politicians into violating aspects of life. He believes that anyone who lives out The Word and wants to live their lives by 'proper life principles' and would like to see society as a whole governed by these 'proper principles of life preservation and flourishment' is a type of 'fundamental politician' and are his representatives'!

DAR DAR: 'We really are nearing the end of the world as we know it, ey? You told me the last time he dislikes games aswell. What did he have to say about that again?'!

TONY: 'In his opinion games involve putting oneself under unnecessary pressure to achieve completely inanimate outcomes. He detests the way sports fans have made a 'religion' out of their favourite teams and also knows that fans referring to their idols as God is extremely dangerous. He says it is idol worship and this is not just a sin but a violation of one of the Commandments and not only is it a violation of a Commandment but of the very first one. That's how serious an issue it is particularly when it's on the Sabbath and that's a violation of another Commandment. Yet again, he said when Yahweh raises him up to be one of His witnesses, he'll be tormenting those playing games'!

DAR DAR: 'That would make him extremely disliked. Sport is what a lot of people live for'!

TONY: 'He told me that he knows how unpopular it will make him but it doesn't bother him as the world is not one last sign to him, he is one last sign to the inhabitants of this planet. He revealed if you reject him, the probability is that you'll be left behind on earth while all sorts of judgements are being cast'!

DAR DAR: 'This is heavy stuff. Tell me more, Tony'!

TONY: 'He advised me there will be no more time for betting offices. He says betting is false prophecy and that not every bet put on by every person proves to be accurate and that even a winning bet is just guess work. He continued that if it was genuine prophecy, there would be no doubt about the outcome. It's false prophetic prediction and thus prophecy in the Lord's Name i.e. it is an offence against Him and it is in His Name because nothing in this universe is outside the dominion of his control or mind-frame. He says it is bad for your health and that 'the false prophet' will endorse 'the beast's' proponentisation of it'!

DAR DAR: 'I don't know what to say. This is mental. But it's the reality mate'!

TONY: 'He says the reality is that sometimes the reality is that the reality shouldn't be the reality! He asserts that he will be proving the world wrong and is probably the main reason why the feminine side of God will once again be greatly revered as he believes men are largely responsible for having, with too much reason, reasoned the unreasonable into reason and a lot of it is philosophied nonsense'!

DAR DAR: 'It sounds to me like feminists would love this guy'!

TONY: 'He says feminists are probably right regarding certain things but are wrong for thinking males and females are the same. He believes men and women could be the same as spirits but while we reside on earth we are part-animal and there are thus intended natural differences. He says Yahweh is part-masculine and part-feminine and that it's just worldliness manifesting itself in either gender which detracts from the individuals' respective masculinity or femininity. He basically feels we are all our own speciality and reflect the love, righteousness and glory of Yahweh irrespective of our gender and animal-type'!

DAR DAR: 'Oh, I see. That's interesting'!

TONY: 'He just said it's more about being an advocate of spiritual power regardless of whether it manifests itself in males or females rather than be a materialistically-orientated, worldly power-player which is a mixture of dragging others down or compressing them i.e. the bad traditions of our forefathers'!

DAR DAR: 'Did he have to say anything else about 'the son of perdition' and 'the false prophet'?'!

TONY: 'As I told you the last time we talked, Francis is that last pope who will be usurped, replaced or succeeded by 'the false prophet' whom 'the son of perdition' will turn to as a way of trying to get back up in order to deceive the world that he is doing the right thing. He says 'the beast' will probably act confused relative to deception when doing so and 'the false prophet' will give him his backing and probably try to convince people there will be plenty of time for these things. He says the Lord Himself advised that it is His own teaching that is the rock on which the church is built. He revealed that when Jesus said to Peter 'thou art Peter and upon this rock I build my church' He was letting Peter know that it's the teaching which He gave during His public ministry which is the rock. Afterall, who gave who the keys. It was Jesus who gave Peter the keys to life (i.e. the teaching) and no pope has ever been any sort of a rock although they've very probably all been good people and have had a lot of profound things to say. However, all Christ ever did was quote

Old Testament and speak in the parables Yahweh educated Him to. The Roman Catholic church has added things in throughout the centuries and while he accepts some of it may be accurate, he's certain not all of it is. He doesn't think the pope is infallible if what he says lies outside of what the Lord taught. He professes that he is the Counsellor and he doesn't even regard what he teaches himself to be infallible although Jesus prophesised his existence and asked for people to pay attention to what he would have to say to the churches. He thinks it's time we re-established Jesus Christ in Christianity'!

DAR DAR: 'I don't know what to say to all of this. It's powerful stuff'!

TONY: 'It is. To sum it all up, he quoted Scripture by saying 'knowledge of this world is folly with The Lord' and 'you can't be a friend of this world and be a friend of God'. It will be the end for empty religious doctrine, secular politics, materialistic greed, a lot of games, betting offices and possibly some other things that people accept as licit. However, he is also in knowledge of another thing that he has heard which he doesn't know whether is Scripture-based or not that goes 'the world has been established, it cannot be moved''!

DAR DAR: 'He's going to be fecking sorting it all out when Yahweh raises him up to be one of His witnesses though, isn't he?'!

TONY: 'It's very possible alright mate! He says that 'the beast' is going to be charismatic during the forty two months he has power but after he martyrs him, he will be possessed and probably try to make people feel guilty for having abided by the traditions of our forefathers (including worldly

74

and secular accessories), take the good out of the efforts we have made to enhance our own and one another's life quality and use the life which things exude to make people feel guilty and whip up dissension among brethren. He thinks we are going to have to learn to re-establish the truth within ourselves because very soon it's going to be a case of 'if you deal with the nonsense, you will be driven insane and if you don't deal with it, the son of perdition will try to walk all over you"!

DAR DAR: 'What do you mean by the life which things exude?'!

TONY: 'He was telling me that material things don't have the breath of life in them like humans and animals but they have the 'creative life source' which brought them into existence in the first place that surrounds them and, because they do exist, have life they exude which he will perversify to antagonise people. You are meant to centre God only but he's prophesising he'll be a self-centred, power-player who'll try to create a power vacuum of ego-centric worldliness a lot of which will be based on the material but he might show regard for the natural too as a part of his deception because he likes to believe he brought it all into existence i.e. he has these delusions he's God'!

DAR DAR: 'That's what he's foretelling. Goodness me'!

TONY: 'He's saying the rapture, where all the saints will be caught up to Heaven, is going to have to happen soon and that it will be shortly after that the son of perdition is going to come on the scene. He's believing that it's sticking out like a sore thumb and that he is going to have to fill that vacant seat number six hundred and sixty six in the European parliament. He thinks it's really sad that just because he'll do things with the financial world that some are going to think he's performing miracles but he says the man is Lucifer incarnate and isn't capable of performing miracles of any sort because he's evil. He believes his real goal is to heavily induce the world economy into eventual ruin so he can cause all the mayhem during that time and basically start 'the great seven year tribulation' as has been prophesised. He says the materialistic order which has been established will be precisely what will enable 'the beast' to crush spirits as Jesus prophesised'!

DAR DAR: 'Sweet Jesus'!

TONY: 'He's prophesising that during 'the son of perdition's' forty two months of power a lot of people will buy into the materialistic prosperity thing but when he is resurrected, it will become apparent to the inhabitants of planet earth that it is superficial. He's kind of expecting that the lack of demand for material things thereafter might contribute to the various markets crashing'!

DAR DAR: 'This is some serious revelation stuff, ey?'!

TONY: 'Yeah. 'I dislike people who are intent on having power over others' is what he revealed. 'It's more important to have power with fellow human beings' is the attitude of real people regardless of what social class you are from according to him. He says we all fall short of God's standards and no one individual is the sole blessee of wisdom'!

DAR DAR: 'Yeah, I agree with that'!

TONY: 'He says his favourite people are those who are ordinary but have the integrity or those who have the integrity but maintain their ordinariness'!

DAR DAR: 'Very good. You told me the last time we talked that he says he was abused by these evil media men. Did he say anything else about his experience?'!

TONY: 'Yeah, I remember. He says these evil media men were relentlessly trespassing upon his life, invading his privacy and violating his very being. He's maintaining they were putting up a front of being on his side but he knew they were empowering and taking the side of those who were being cruel to him in order to further frustrate him in the interim. He's also saying they were abusing those whom he was coming into contact with. Maybe the people whom he was associating with thought that they were being mistreated too but he knew what was going on because the media involvement in his life had been going on since he was a baby. There were all sorts of direct and indirect references making him a prisoner in his circumstances. He stated that by abusing and belittling the people he cared for was taking away from his quality of life and adding to his own suffering'!

DAR DAR: 'Good grief. Had he anything else to reveal?'!

TONY: 'He had. He's maintaining these men knew what music he liked and while those songs were being played over the airwaves, they were cut off and interrupted in an abusive manner. He confesses that he knows that practically everybody likes music and that some would have liked the songs he favoured too but all the songs he liked were either referred to or cut off. He's maintaining these men de-proponentised him having any sort of quality of life'!

DAR DAR: 'If this is true, he must have really suffered throughout his life'!

TONY: 'He says he has been through mental and emotional torture and it's a miracle he's still alive particularly with him coming down with his illness, going on to medication and not knowing what he was taking it for, coming off the medication, relapsing, going through psychotic episodes and now recovering from his last episode over the past eleven years having finally got a clinical diagnosis'!

DAR DAR: 'The poor bloke. With schizophrenia you struggle with the media because of the disorder too, don't you?'

TONY: 'That's what he was telling me. As I advised you the last time, he's saying the media know who he is and the really sad thing is that while he was growing into the mind-frame where he was becoming the media-God he is, the nature of the relationship he is meant to have with broadcasters was distorted all simultaneous with him coming down with the psychosis. He was saying that he has had to deal with what has being coming through radio and television broadcasts over the last nineteen years not knowing what he was influencing while it was only apparent to some areas who it is he is. But now they all know and everything is being straightened out'!

DAR DAR: 'Feck me. I don't know what you mean by distorted though'!

TONY: 'He revealed to me that as his mind was beginning to really develop, the nature of the relationship he is meant to have with media people was being distorted. Beforehand, his belief was that media people were just entities but with the little bit of paranoia he was worried that media people were regular individuals who could be approached and empowered through to get at him via their broadcasts'!

DAR DAR: 'Well he is a paranoid schizophrenic, isn't he?'!

TONY: 'I know. He says he accepts this but that that's what the really unfortunate thing for him is. He advised me that he was growing into his mind-frame and that the media are supposed to be serving him but he was worried that some of them were developing a negative opinion as the negative opinions others had of him was spreading to the media and they were dealing with him when in retrospect the media were aware of how those whom he was coming into contact with were deluding themselves and it was the people who were persecuting him whom the media were sorting out'!

DAR DAR: 'I don't know what to say that. I'm fecking speechless'!

TONY: 'He told me it was total confusion for him and he never really convinced himself the media were abusing him but with the way things had happened, with some people he associated with and the forces of coincidence making him paranoid it was always a possibility. He just didn't know what to think'!

DAR DAR: 'But that's just what it was, coincidences as you said'!

TONY: 'Yeah, but he doesn't look at 'forces of coincidence' as coincidence, he looks at them as forces and he really believes a powerful evil spirit entity was playing games with his mind and trying to perversify everything for him'!

DAR DAR: 'This is blowing my mind, Tony'!

TONY: 'Another thing he revealed was that when he was growing into his mind-frame, he began to trust these evil media men. He continued that he's certain Jesus Christ knew this would happen and was greatly upset by it but now due to schizophrenia, a Godly mind-frame and regression he's moved into his past and he realises it was going on all his life and that they were purposely positioned to destroy his welfare'!

DAR DAR: 'This really is powerful stuff mate. He's had to deal with a lot, ey?'!

TONY: 'He has. He informed me that all the media are on his side now but it was torture for him having to deal with what the evil media men knew about him too'!

DAR DAR: 'I've heard of 'the battle-field of the mind' but this takes the biscuit mate'!

TONY: 'Yeah, you're right. He told me he has been through mental and emotional torture, as I just said, and it's a miracle he's still alive. He says the reason the media know about everything going on in his life is because they have someone or something he sent into the world so that it would be there to serve him when he decided to come to planet earth. He revealed to me that it's basically an influence from the supernatural realm which is furnishing the media with the knowledge of all the actualities going on in his life which they are aware of'!

DAR DAR: 'Is there no wonder he was confused'!

TONY: 'He was telling me for a good while he thought people were going off and furnishing the media of his actualities and he was having difficulty in functioning because he didn't really know why it was happening. He says he hadn't quite grown into his media-God mind-frame and the nature of the relationship was distorted'!

DAR DAR: 'All that on top of these evil media men abusing him too, right?'!

TONY: 'True. He says he has his opinions about what was going on but would rather keep them to himself. How could they know about everything going on with him when they were nowhere near his vicinity?'!

DAR DAR: 'Goodness me'!

TONY: 'He says for the majority of his life he has been a repressed prisoner in his very being and circumstances. They even knew at least some of his thoughts according to him'!

DAR DAR: 'I'm stuck for words. I've heard some things in my time but nothing as powerful as this'!

TONY: 'He was also saying these men were making him feel guilty for the temptations he suffered from which were completely beyond his control and he may not even have succumbed to'!

DAR DAR: 'This is mental'!

TONY: 'I know. He says what's unfortunate for him is that not only did he reap what he hadn't sewn but that which he had always been the victim of anyway. He continued some of those he was coming into contact with in his life in general had possibly felt the abuse by these media men but had never truly been the intended target. I did tell you the last time he harbours the belief these men were trying to turn everybody against one another particularly putting a strain on the relationship between the genders while empowering the materialistically inclined and trying to dictate that people feed their materialistic egos, exact retribution and become power-players and false prophets i.e. basically induce people into doing the wrong things with their freedom. That which will hurt themselves and others and get them on the wrong side of Yahweh and Yeshua because they don't know the truth'!

DAR DAR: 'If this is all true, I don't know how this bloke has survived'!

TONY: 'He told me survive is all he's done for the last nineteen years. He says he has hardly done any living during this time. He let me know he has been treated very cruelly by people including being made a scapegoat by females. However, his illness is possibly the cruellest thing of all'!

DAR DAR: 'So not only has he been struggling with his relationship with the media but with people he was coming into contact with too. All simultaneous with him becoming unwell. This is fecking awful'!

TONY: 'It is. I feel so sorry for the guy as he's as innocent. He was told he has the mental age of a one year old for goodness sake. He said he never knew what to make of people's unnatural behaviour towards him. He said he accepts there were probably times when people were trying to help him (and for that he is thankful) but it was like giving someone cough medicine for a broken limb. All he needed at the time was to find out the nature of his relationship with the media. As I just told you, he says the nature of this relationship had been distorted while he was just about developing into the media-God he has become. He said he knows he is probably being a little paranoid but it was as if some people whom he came into contact with were even more aware of his circumstances than he was of his own. It was total confusion for him'!

DAR DAR: 'I don't know what to say to all of this. All this concurrent with him struggling with and not knowing fully the nature of his relationship with the media while the evil men were violating him and perversifying his character and circumstances as you told me the last time'!

TONY: 'He asserts that the more the material secular world order grows, the more mental and emotional damage it will do to him and, because he lives inside others, add to others' suffering too. But they may not realise it for all people know is prosperity. He also revealed the more materially self-sufficient the world and people become, the greater the difficulty the world will have in accepting him and treating him properly'!

DAR DAR: 'I see. Maybe what he says about these evil media men trying to induce people into feeding their materialistic egos, exacting retribution and becoming power-players and false prophets is true'!

TONY: 'It could be accurate alright. He says he has had the horribleness of his adult life hanging over him since he was an infant and it has always been very difficult for him to stay on the rails throughout his life because of the treatment he had been, was and always knew he would be on the receiving end of from the media and the people he knew he'd come into contact with'!

DAR DAR: 'That's sad'!

TONY: 'He informed me that he was making mistakes during his early adult life in particular because he had always known he'd go through something very distressing, disturbing, cruel and painful. He detected in his spirit that the persecution he had been subjected to through the media wasn't going to dissipate but only grow, intensify and get worse which it did eventually'!

DAR DAR: 'Sounds to me like he has psychic abilities'!

TONY: 'It does to me too. He says he's a prophet. Yet again, he asserted that he was probably being a little paranoid but it was as if he's always been deprived of all his rights which fully evidences Jesus Christ's prophecy that the world would not be able to accept him. I agreed with him when he argued that you have to be allowed to fight your corner when you feel like you are being dictated to. It wasn't rebellious-ness or disobedience in any way which was probably what was being construed by the evil media men. They are the ones who are rebellious and disobedient'!

DAR DAR: 'Yeah. I've experienced some abusive things through sections of the media over the years too. He feels he was always the intended target, doesn't he?'!

TONY: 'He does believe in many cases he was alright'!

DAR DAR: 'Well if 'the beast' is currently on this planet and he's the Counsellor, it's a no-brainer for sure'!

TONY: 'He says a lot of his fears have been realised, practically everything that could have gone wrong did and that his prophetic abilities have been abused'!

DAR DAR: 'But the evil media men have been removed from their positions according to him now, ey?'!

TONY: 'Yeah. He told me he's going to put his experiences in a book. He has a funny feeling that one day the 'Marjorie Daw' will get involved. He feels the prophets knew this would happen and that this is where the term 'throw the book at them' came from as the evil media men will probably try make out he is mad! 'As mad as a box of mentally ill frogs drinking whiskey which has been spiked with bleach' as he put it'!

DAR DAR: 'I never have and probably never will hear the likes of this again'!

TONY: 'We'll see what lies in store for planet earth over the coming decade or so. Finally, he was telling me he has had martyrdom awaiting him since he was two years old and that there is a picture in his house where he is crying and looking upwards. He says while this photograph was been taken he was prophesising his resurrection and acting out what a lot of people will be doing when he goes off to Heaven in a blaze of glory (as is referred to in the Book of Revelations). I told you about the dream he said he had the last time, didn't I?'!

DAR DAR: 'You did but run it by me again'!

TONY: 'He says in this dream he had a vision from what he believes was The Last Supper and that Jesus Christ was checking Himself out in a mirror. He believes this was the Lord prophesising his existence and was advising him he is like a proverbial mirror himself and while Jesus liked His own reflection there would be some who would look into his face and not like what they saw of themselves. Although another aspect of this dream could have been the Lord relieving him of what guilt He was prophesising he would feel for being vain because He knew he would be induced into checking out his reflection a lot. Another thing Jesus might have being doing is encouraging him to have a more positive self-image because He knew the way the media would treat him and that the way they would conduct themselves would induce him into not seeing himself as a nice-looking man and good person. He says they have always been the cause of him having low self-esteem and a negative self-image. He advised me that certain sections of the media have been making him live in the past and have had him reflecting too respectfully on his problems'!

DAR DAR: 'Oh, right'!

TONY: 'He said the next thing he experienced in this dream was a vision from the future. He informed me he was covered in glory, could hear people crying and a lady called out his name. He says this is what will happen within moments of him being resurrected along with the other witness. Oh, while I think of it he mentioned some things Christ said at The Last Supper which are repeated during Mass'!

DAR DAR: 'What things?'!

TONY: 'Jesus said 'stay awake, stay sober', 'by their fruit you shall know them', 'you'll be made a prisoner' and 'and if they take your life'!

DAR DAR: 'These things relate to him, don't they?'

TONY: 'He thinks they might be. The 'stay awake, stay sober' was something some people who know him would understand is about. He thinks 'by their fruit you shall know them' could be in relation to the evil media men who made him a prisoner in his circumstances and very being. That's what he believes the 'you'll be made a prisoner' bit is about although he's a little scared he might be incarcerated for being a non-conformist. The 'and if they take your life' is the fact that he would one day be martyred. He's saying he's accepted this since he was a baby and it's what Jesus might have been referring to'!

DAR DAR: 'Well, as I said to you the last time, this bloke is going to be diagnosed as either mad or a genius but you told me a professional advised him he's a genius. If he does go off to Heaven in a blaze of glory, I'll tip my hat to him for having proved the world wrong'!

TONY: 'Yeah. He maintains it will have had to have been one of the greatest days in the history of mankind and planet earth. Talk to you again soon. I'll let you know if he tells me any more'!

DAR DAR: 'Cheers. If it does happen, it will be a day never to be forgotten alright. It could be a real tear-jerker. I'll see you later pal'!